Foreword

My life as a specialist nursery grower started in 1984 a few years before Louise took her diploma in Garden Design at The English Gardening School.

I have made many gardening friends and enjoyed numerous chats about their gardens and how well plants have thrived or not in various situations. One fact that is clear to me is that plants do not read the books which pronounce the conditions they need and may flourish in very different environments as Louise has found in her garden. For me the greatest achievement of my profession is to encourage gardeners to seek and grow beautiful and interesting plants which are suited to their garden environment.

In this lovely book Louise has selected many of my favourite plants for richness of texture and colour as well as providing nutrition for our insect and bird populations in the form of nectar, pollen and berries. Since 2000, I have been an RHS Trials judge and am delighted that Louise has chosen many plants with an Award of Garden Merit (AGM). Although not all plants have been trialled to date and new cultivars are constantly produced, the AGM is a valuable guide and short cut for gardeners to use when selecting plants.

Louise has produced an erudite, well researched book with indisputable hands-on knowledge as well as a beautiful photographic record of her favourite plants in the garden she and Rob created over the last 30 years. I thoroughly recommend it.

Marina Christopher
(October'20)

Contents

About

A few years ago, a great gardening friend asked me if I would write a column for the blog that she and her two sisters had just set up, The3Growbags. Of course, I said 'yes'; plants and gardens are part of what I am, and this new writing venture would give me another excuse to immerse myself further into my hobby.

Already an avid gardener, I took a Diploma in Garden Design with The English Gardening School at the Chelsea Physic Garden in the late 80s. This set me up twofold: on the course I met my husband, Rob, who loves gardens and the greater landscape as much as I do, and together we have created our garden from scratch, over the last thirty years. It also helped me to understand that a garden is not just composed of plants: it needs to be supported by logical concepts and a meaningful 'skeleton'.

This booklet is a distillation of some of those writings, taken from over the last four years. I have called it 'A Plant for Each Week of the Year' because it is not only flowers that I have chosen; I get as much enjoyment from the silhouette of a tree in winter, a good architectural evergreen or a frosted seedhead as I do from a beautiful flower. This is not a guide of what to plant and when, but rather a collection of what inspires me the most at that time of year.

You may notice the Royal Horticultural Society's 'Award of Garden Merit' logo amongst many of my choices — it's their quality "seal of approval that the plant performs reliably in the garden". There are tens of thousands of plants available to buy in the UK, and sometimes the choice is overwhelming. To help you, keep an eye out for this little logo: it's always reassuring because, believe me, it's well earned!

A final word about the seasons and the very diverse climates, soils and temperatures to be found on these islands that we inhabit: they differ hugely from one end of the land to the other and, indeed, from one end of our village to the other. The consequences are that what works for us on heavy clay in Sussex, may differ wildly from what can be grown elsewhere, but I hope that among my choices are some that work for everyone.

Louise

To Rob

Parrotia persica

Persian ironwood

I **first saw *Parrotia persica* (as a group of three) in the winter garden at Polesden Lacey and wanted one immediately; the sight of those deep-crimson flowers erupting from bare branches was captivating.** As with many flowers at this time of year you must get up close to appreciate their beauty but then that is the enjoyment of being in the winter garden: it is a stroll of discovery of tiny details on a cold day, as opposed to a blast of unmissable colour in the heat of summer.

The Persian ironwood is a hardy, deciduous, upwardly-spreading tree and a member of the same family as the witch hazel's, the Hamamelidaceae. It is often multi-stemmed and although it needs no regular pruning, after a few years it may benefit from the careful removal of some of the lower limbs to allow more light in and to raise the crown. There's no escaping the fact that it's a big tree with a height of 6 to 8 metres after 25 years.

It has a second trick up its sleeve and that is its spectacular autumn display. Every hue of yellow, orange, red, crimson and purple is there and when the leaves finally drop we have a Persian carpet covering the grass underneath.

Daphne laureola

spurge laurel

Many winter-flowering shrubs are unassuming, their blooms subtle, and many are fragrant; most often you catch the scent on the air before you see the flowers.

Daphne laureola, commonly known as the spurge laurel, is one of two native daphnes found in the UK and it is easy to grow and utterly dependable — unlike some of the others in the genus that we know!

It has attractive, polished evergreen leaves which arrange themselves as rosettes, forming a neat dome about a metre high, and rather wider, after many years. The effect is reminiscent of the euphorbia family, however, Daphne laureola is much longer lived. The clusters of pale-yellow or lime-green flowers appear in late winter and are deliciously scented.

It won't stop you in your tracks, but I have come to respect this daphne. Tolerant of almost any aspect, from deep shade to full sun, and everything in between, it makes few demands in terms of upkeep. It is always admired when in flower and is very easy to propagate, either by taking cuttings or by pinning down one of the lower branches with a heavy stone, where it will easily root.

Crocus tommasinianus

early crocus

The big reward for me, gardening in January, is not only getting ahead of things while it's relatively quiet but also coming across all of the tiny signs that spring is just around the corner. My plant this week may seem an obvious choice, but it never fails to stop me in my tracks with its delicate lilac flowers and their brilliant orange anthers. The same can be said for the bumble bees, who welcome the rich source of early pollen. Frail as the flowers may look, it is a resilient little plant and copes well in quite tough surroundings amongst other plants and grass.

We planted ours originally along the side of a path and their corms have now multiplied and they have generously seeded themselves further into the grass: they are the perfect naturalisers and are among the first in the genus to flower. This crocus manages well in dappled shade, but full sun will bring out its best.

Crocus tommasinianus is native to many parts of eastern Europe, but it is equally happy growing in a pot on your balcony — so there is no excuse!

Anisodontea 'El Royo'

African mallow 'El Royo'

The first *Anisodontea* that I ever grew was *A. capensis,* which is less hardy, less showy, and smaller in all respects but very charming nonetheless. Then I came across *A.* 'El Royo', another member of the mallow family, which has much larger, clear-pink flowers with dark centres, and it blooms best, most unusually, in autumn and winter.

It is a hardy evergreen subshrub reaching about 1.5 metres. So far mine has withstood a string of quite hard frosts; it just keeps on going. It has an airy habit and will perform best in a sunny, well-drained spot, with minimum fuss — a hard prune in mid spring will set it up well for the rest of the year.

I should point out that if you go online to see what others say about this plant, you will discover an even split between naming it 'El Royo' and 'El Rayo'. I am firmly in the former camp after reading about it in Bob Brown's hugely informative (and funny) catalogue, 'Cotswold Garden Flowers', and as far as I am concerned, what he says — goes! He also gives most plants a score out of ten and this little gem quite rightly scores nine.

It grows happily in a large pot and can therefore be placed wherever you will get maximum enjoyment.

Chaenomeles x superba 'Pink Lady'

Japanese quince 'Pink Lady'

Every gardener is familiar with the ornamental quince. They are easy to grow, very hardy, can stand freely or be trained tightly against a wall, come in many colours — some more familiar than others — and are tolerant of almost any soil type. What is often not pointed out is the ability of some of them to thrive in almost total shade and this particular one, 'Pink Lady', does just that.

What's more, it must be the earliest of them all to flower. Ours tends to start in the middle of January and is very prolific. The tiny, dark pink buds burst from bare branches, open to a clear mid-pink, and are stunning. The flowers positively glow in what would otherwise be a rather murky corner under trees at this time of the year.

We also grow *C. speciosa* 'Nivalis' which is a very old variety with beautiful snow-white flowers that show up well on a north wall and another specimen in our garden grows happily in the dappled shade of a cherry tree.

Being members of the *Rosaceae* family, which includes many fruit trees, they are accepting of hard pruning and I have seen them very effectively, and sometimes meticulously, trained around doorways and windows.

The fruits, which arrive in the autumn, are not plentiful but they are extremely high in pectin and make delicious jellies.

Salix fargesii

Farges willow

During periods of hard frost, it is not difficult to find stunning subjects to admire as you wander around the garden; every stem, seedhead and leaf is enhanced by the sparkling white dusting of a hoar frost.

The challenging days are when it's grey, dismal and the light levels are at their lowest. But even then, I know that there will always be something to brighten things up and at this time of the year I look to *Salix fargesii,* which we have planted at the edge of our pond.

There are about 400 species of deciduous willow, their main season of interest being late winter and early spring and most have either distinctive colourful stems, showy catkins or interesting foliage. Some have all three!

However, the conspicuous, bright red buds of *S. fargesii,* set against its glossy dark stems are hard to beat. For the average-sized garden it makes for an excellent choice, seldom reaching more than 2 metres in height. It is also fairly slow-growing and with careful pruning (it doesn't need much), will form an attractive, open shrub.

It seems almost too obvious to mention, but you couldn't do better than to grow a carpet of snowdrops underneath.

Helleborus argutifolius

Syn. Helleborus corsicus, Helleborus lividus subsp. corsicus, Corsican hellebore, holly-leaved hellebore

That description, 'holly-leaved', could put you off, but don't let it. It isn't prickly, rather that the handsome leathery leaves have a gently serrated edge. They have an almost metallic sheen which perfectly sets off the clusters of palest apple-green, cup-shaped flowers which are very long-lasting. They will still be there as spring drifts into summer. If you want it to self-seed then leave the ageing flowerheads; if not, there comes a time when you will want to tidy it up (usually around mid-May) and you can cut off each of these, right down to the base.

This hellebore, one of the largest and most imposing of the genus, is native to both Corsica and Sardinia. In Corsica, it can be found in many different habitats, from shoreline to woodland to mountainside. I have seen it growing among shaded boulders where it relishes escaping from the heat; interestingly, in our garden, it chooses to self-seed happily in an area of east-facing paving.

This evergreen perennial, attaining from 60 to 100cm in height, is clearly very adaptable and for simplicity of planting, needs nothing more than a drift of *Narcissus* 'February Gold' at its side.

Teucrium fruticans

tree germander

I don't really linger in the garden in February, but I do make a quick round every day whatever the weather, and love to notice all of the subtle changes. The best time for this is in the early morning after a sharp frost: I never fail to be amazed by the entrancing transformations made by it and am reminded not to be overhasty in cutting down the stems of many perennials and grasses in particular.

There is one plant which looks particularly good right now — and quite unscathed by the -6°C a few days ago — and that is the shrubby germander, *Teucrium fruticans.* Its curious, asymmetrical blue flowers (which are meant to appear in the summer months) are set off by stiff, almost ghostly white stems and silvery grey foliage. It's an unusual sight at this time of the year for most grey-leaved plants undoubtedly look their best in the summer.

Being native to the Mediterranean, *T. fruticans* loves sunshine and good drainage, and can easily attain 1.5 metres in all directions. However, don't lose heart if your plot is on the smaller side as it is happily (and best) pruned in spring and can indeed be clipped quite hard; in mild areas I've seen it grown as a hedge. Alternatively, there is a dwarf form called 'Compactum' which I haven't grown, but it could be the perfect answer if space is at a premium.

Ficaria verna 'Brazen Hussy'

Syn. Ranunculus ficaria 'Brazen Hussy'
lesser celandine 'Brazen Hussy'

William Wordsworth wrote no less than three poems in celebration of our rather plain native lesser celandine — can you imagine the raptures if he had come across 'Brazen Hussy'? Its polished, heart-shaped, bronze-black leaves form a ground-hugging mound from which the golden-yellow flowers cheerfully shine out as if to declare that spring really is on its way.

Closely related to the buttercup, this tuberous rooted perennial takes me by surprise every year: one minute the earth is bare, the next it pops up as if by magic. The lesser celandine is summer dormant which means that after flowering it completely disappears.

At this stage, I should point out that, in our garden at least, 'Brazen Hussy' has none of the self-spreading capabilities of its native cousin, although I can imagine that there might exist gardens where conditions allow it to become invasive.

We can be sure that it was named by Christopher Lloyd, but was it discovered by him, his mother Daisy, or his head gardener? Whoever it was, they spotted a little jewel!

MARCH

Iris lazica

Lazistan iris

This plant is not to be confused with *Iris unguicularis* which I wrote about in my column in February 2017. Although closely related, their needs differ in many respects and for that reason it is well worth giving it a plug as this week's plant.

Iris lazica is native to coastal areas of the Black Sea in Turkey and Georgia and, unlike the Algerian iris which needs a hot, dry spot in poor soil, this one positively thrives in semi-shade (or even full shade) and preferably a little damp. Unlike *Iris unguicularis* which flowers from November onwards, it flowers later in March. So, if you grow both species, you will have a succession of lilac blue flowers for at least five months of the year. The leaves of *I. lazica* are similarly strappy but less untidy than its cousin's and the beautiful flowers seem to hunker down into the foliage, while still standing out.

If you are an impatient gardener, then this one might not be for you. I planted ours several years ago at the base of an *Elaeagnus umbellata* and it had a bit of a sulk for the first couple of seasons. Now, however, it is a mature clump, a circle of some 60cm across and the display of flowers seems to get better with each year that passes.

Bergenia emeiensis

The name *Bergenia* might provoke a little shudder in some people, so I hope my photograph has instantly caught your attention because this one is about as far as one can get from the murky purple-pink offerings most commonly seen in spring.

B. emeiensis is a compact, hardy, evergreen plant — a species with pure white, elegant flowers on pinkish stems, above shiny mid-green leaves that are more oval than wide. It does not need any special attention, indeed, mine is on the edge of a raised bed and could be deemed to be in too dry a spot for a plant that originates from damp woodland.

This is not a plant that is commonly available and that's because it was only relatively recently introduced, in the 1980's. However, don't let that put you off, you can always grow it from seed. It is available from Jelitto Perennial Seeds whose germination rates are outstanding.

While I am on the subject of bergenias, I must mention *B. ciliata*, another favourite of mine that has very low-growing, pale-pink flowers above gnarled, almost bare, stems at this time of year. However, as the season progresses, its fantastic, vast, and hairy leaves take centre stage and make a real architectural statement, especially on the corner of a bed where its growth need not be restricted.

Ribes sanguineum 'White Icicle'

flowering currant 'White Icicle'

In this most magical of months when there is so much happening in the garden, I want to put in a word for a member of the currant family. All too often the only one available is the very dull pink *R. sanguineum*. You could look out for *Ribes* 'Pulborough Scarlet' which, as its name suggests, does have very striking deep pink blooms, but my favourite is the one with snow-white flowers.

Interestingly, almost everywhere you read about 'White Icicle', it says it needs 'full sun'. Well, this is nonsense and I probably wouldn't have time for it if that were the case, for when not in bud (which emerge in a most enticing way towards the end of February) or in flower, its overall appearance is dull and you wouldn't want to waste your best sunny spot.

I have one in deep shade on the north wall of our house and it only sees the sun for half an hour in the very late afternoon. What's more, it is all the more striking for being in the shade where the white pendant flowers positively glow. I have another in dappled shade near an oak tree and its upright habit is the perfect umbrella for any number of spring woodland treasures.

It's a very easy shrub: all it needs is a hard prune after flowering and this keeps it to a more manageable size.

Prunus incisa 'Kojo-no-mai'

cherry 'Kojo-no-mai'

This is undoubtedly a well known and popular cherry, and deservedly so. However, somehow I overlooked it until a few years ago when — right time, right place — I found I had a gap for a spring flowering shrub and it fitted the bill perfectly. Compact, slow growing and twiggy in an architectural sort of way, in early spring it is covered in masses of dainty, white (flushed pink) flowers giving the whole plant an almost ethereal quality. This belies its resilience (it's very hardy) and ease of cultivation. It's also known as the Fuji cherry — how beautiful it must look growing on the misty slopes of Mount Fuji.

Its flowers are subtle, which is more than can be said of some of the brasher pink cherries, and they are all the more striking for appearing on bare twigs. The leaves, with serrated (incised) edges, make their very important contribution later in the year when they take on every imaginable autumnal hue.

It is the perfect choice for a small garden and I'd love to try one in a pot.

As I write this, I have made a note to remind myself to move some chionodoxa, so that next year there will be a carpet of blue underneath our Fuji cherry to complete the picture.

APRIL

Bellevalia romana

Roman hyacinth

My head is telling me that I should be writing about one of the many spring-flowering shrubs that are looking so stunning right now, but my heart is telling me otherwise. This week I'm going for a beautiful yet seldom seen bulb that is such an eye-catching plant despite being quite small (25–30cm) and one that fits seamlessly into the spring tapestry.

Over the years I have bought many interesting plants from Marina Christopher (Phoenix Perennial Plants) and this is one of them. Having just looked up the date of purchase in my garden book, I have noticed that this one was back in 2006. So, to anyone who is wondering if it has an over-enthusiastic 'naturalising' habit — it is after all a relative of muscari — I can only say that for us (on heavy clay) it has been a model participant, only gently increasing. It is completely hardy, easy, very rewarding, and has a lot more charisma than a grape hyacinth.

I collected some seed a couple of years ago and germinated it in pots which I planted out last year. I could probably have scattered the seed where I wanted it and saved a bit of trouble, but it's such a great plant that I wanted to be sure of increasing my stock.

Coronilla valentina subsp. *glauca* 'Citrina'

bastard senna 'Citrina'

It's rather a long title, but names mean everything in the plant world. In this instance 'Citrina' is the vital word because without it you will end up with a plant which, in my opinion, bears rather unappealing chrome-yellow flowers.

This shrub is a member of the pea family. It's a small evergreen (approx. 80cm), but it can reach well over a metre, particularly if planted against a sunny wall. It also makes for a great specimen in a pot. It is a gem — "ten out of ten" says Bob Brown of Cotswold Garden Flowers — and is one of my 'Desert Island Disc' plants. The palest yellow flowers are set off by grey-green foliage and are sweetly fragrant.

The season I most associate with this *Coronilla* is winter, but this year mine waited until early spring and now, in April, it is in full flower and reminding me of the unpredictability and excitement of gardening. So, you are unlikely to get flowers in the summer months, but this is a good time to take cuttings — well worth it for it is not a long-lived plant (three to five years is what I would expect).

Be careful how you prune *Coronilla* and don't do it during a cold snap. It can appear a little untidy at times but be gentle with your secateurs or you will live to regret it.

Exochorda x macrantha 'The Bride'

pearl bush 'The Bride'

We originally planted this eye-catching and bountiful shrub by accident. I had been after an obscure shade loving shrub whose name I have long forgotten, so when this bare rooted, twiggy plant arrived (out of leaf) in late winter, in it went and I didn't give it further thought. Until that is, I spotted the first pearl-like buds appearing in early spring, followed soon after by an abundance of snow-white flowers which had a very long season. I quickly realised that we had been sent the wrong plant, but I didn't care; our *Exochorda* is one of the most glorious unplanned happenings to have occurred in our garden.

Interestingly, it is always listed as needing full sun, or at least only partial shade, whereas ours sits in dappled sun for a scant hour in the early morning and thrives in the shade of a Scots pine for the rest of the day.

This hardy, deciduous shrub is pest- and disease-free and demands nothing more than a hard prune after flowering to keep its arching branches in check. Hardly surprising then to see that it has been awarded the Royal Horticultural Society's 'Award of Garden Merit'.

A word of warning about the cultivar name of 'The Bride': one might imagine that a few twigs of this spring flowering shrub would be the perfect bridal bouquet, but in my experience, it has a very short life as a cut flower and would probably not last the walk down the aisle!

Omphalodes cappadocica *'Cherry Ingram'*

blue-eyed Betty

Thanks to a good friend (and The3Growbags follower) who reminded me of the common name of this week's plant, I have been dipping into a couple of books by Margery Fish. Having read most of them years ago, I am again inspired by her chatty and informative prose and am finding them hard to put down.

A member of the forget-me-not family (*Boraginaceae*), *Omphalodes cappadocica* is a remarkable little plant and its sprays of brilliant blue flowers will enhance and enliven any shady corner for many weeks. Happiest in part or full shade, and preferably damp soil, it seems also to enjoy growing at the side of a path or stone steps, even at the foot of a north wall. Margery writes: "The foliage of O. cappadocica may need a little attention after the winter, but most of the year the pointed leaves are bright glossy green".

Blue-eyed Betty is a 'must have' spring perennial and looks good in combination with so many plants, especially primroses, hellebores, epimediums, and last but by no means least, the unfurling fronds of ferns — pure magic!

Viola labradorica

Labrador violet

Through writing I am always learning something new: this time I had to look up the exact whereabouts of Labrador, Canada, after which this plant is named. In doing so I discovered that this little plant is also native to Greenland, and now I know, and furthermore understand, why it is so resilient.

For me it stands out from other violas on account of its unusual, purple-flushed, heart-shaped foliage which complement the colour of the flowers so perfectly. It is an undemanding plant and will seed itself about gently — a little too gently for me as I could do with a few more if only to dig up and give to friends as it is so often admired.

Easy to please, it seems to love growing in the cracks between paving and occasionally seeds itself (along with everything else) in our gravel paths. Equally happy in sun or shade, it would also make a very pretty specimen in a small terracotta pot: a centrepiece for your outside table, where you could more easily admire the flowers and even deadhead them.

This for me, however, is a step too far — I am too busy feeding my robin.

MAY

Abutilon vitifolium *'Veronica Tennant'*

Thanks are due to middle *Growbag* sister, Laura, who gave me this beautiful shrub as a small cutting a few years ago. I was already growing *Abutilon x suntense* which has stunning deep purpley-blue flowers, but its season is fleeting, whereas 'Veronica Tennant' is in bloom from late spring well into the summer.

This is a strong growing, upright shrub, much hardier than people might think (quite untouched by the recent -2°C here) and the dainty saucer-shaped flowers are a good 8cm across and bees love them! *Abutilon* must have full sun, good drainage and a sheltered spot. Given those conditions, they won't look back.

Now, this leads neatly on to the subject of pruning and eventual height: the general consensus is that *Abutilon* respond well to hard pruning, which is just as well as I like to keep ours within bounds. However, I have always pruned after flowering whereas after some research I see that I should be doing it in early spring — so take your pick. 'Veronica Tennant' is said to reach 4 metres but mine never has the chance to get beyond head height.

Clematis 'Black Tea'

If I wake up in the night and can't get back to sleep, I take a mental tour of the garden and as it's May I might start by counting clematis. I get as far as *C.* 'Black Tea': beyond a shadow of a doubt, it deserves to be this week's star plant and can only be described as 'sumptuous'. It's not just the depth of colour and subtle variations as the light changes that makes it stand out, the flower's petals have an amazing velvety texture. It grows to 6 to 8 foot and is a prolific flowerer.

It wasn't until the second half of the nineteenth century that clematis began to be reinvented, hybridised, and new ones were being introduced to the UK from all over the globe. 'Black Tea', however, is a relatively recent creation from Japan in 1995.

We should plant more clematis especially in smaller gardens because, being vertical, the space they take up is minimal; I have a friend who grows over twenty in her 50 by 25 foot garden.

A final word about pot size: I almost never buy one in anything larger than a 9cm pot. This has several advantages: they are very quick and easy to plant, can be tucked into a space where those huge deep pots just won't fit, they are very quick to establish (I've never had a failure) and they are cheap. That's why I have so many — three for the price of one!

So, I should be asleep before I've finished counting…

Geranium sylvaticum 'Album'

wood cranesbill 'Album'

There are well over 400 species in the genus *Geranium*, and so when it comes to choosing one for that precious spot in your garden, it pays to do a little research and — above all — be selective. It is oh-so-easy to be seduced by the one that happens to be in flower as you pass it in your local nursery or garden centre, but a spontaneous purchase can be a cause for regret later. It might turn out to be too tall, too floppy, too thuggish or too sparing in its flowers. For me at least, the white wood cranesbill fits the bill.

The Latin word *'sylvaticum'* means 'of woodland'. It therefore follows that my plant this week is very tolerant of shade and indeed it is its preferred spot. The plentiful, pure white flowers are held well above the fresh green divided leaves, lighting up any dark corner. Its habit is noticeably upright, it is clump-forming and easy to grow. After flowering, try cutting the whole plant back and you might get a second crop.

Heuchera 'Brown Finch'

coral bells 'Brown Finch'

At this time of the year, almost every time I walk around the garden something new is beginning to flower and my attention is caught by the colour and exuberance of it all: roses, clematis, euphorbias, iris, peonies — the list is endless. However, this week I am going for 'subtle'; if you want flamboyance, there is always the Chelsea Flower Show!

Walk into most garden centres (not nurseries) and you will be regaled with rows of different heucheras. All those garish, unnatural foliage colours almost give me a headache, it's as if there is a competition to find the most lurid hue. My subject is not so noticeable, but it has a quiet, dependable presence and our garden would be poorer without it.

Dappled shade is where I like to grow 'Brown Finch' and it seems to be particularly good at coping under shrubs and trees which is always a useful attribute. Its unusual terracotta coloured flowers rise elegantly (to 60cm) above cool, silver mottled foliage. They are long-lasting and a magnet for bees, whose presence not only gives us much pleasure but they are quite simply, vital to life itself.

Rosa 'Souvenir du Docteur Jamain'

climbing

There are so many beautiful roses out right now, so how on earth do I choose just one?

No rose is perfect and my favourite this week shares certain less attractive traits with many others. Let's face it: few roses look their best after days of rain and this one is no exception — it really sulks. Then there is the dying process which can be untidy at best or downright unsightly at worst. But in so many other respects, 'Souvenir du Docteur Jamain' is a winner.

First off, it is one of the most suitable for a north facing wall: its rich, claret-coloured, velvety flowers are deeply fragrant, but they tend to fade in full sun so their position of choice would be in dappled shade. Being almost thornless is another 'plus'.

This sumptuous rose is a climbing hybrid perpetual and was bred in 1865 by Francois Lacharme and was apparently a great favourite of Vita Sackville-West. The first and main flush of flowers is in June, but deadheading will give you a second, lesser flush in late summer. It reaches 6 to 8 foot in height and its new growth is particularly pliable so tie it in to as near horizontal as possible, which will encourage a greater number of flowers.

Clematis 'Belle of Woking'

I bought this clematis three years ago: a strong little plant in a 9cm pot and it has never looked back. I mention the size of the pot because I find that these young plants, although given their size are a little vulnerable and need a bit of extra protection initially, soon take off and establish well — a bit like planting whips instead of more mature trees. Also, being in such small pots, they are much easier to fit into an already overcrowded bed.

So — big hole, lots of organic matter and food, a large drink, and a slab over the top to help keep the roots cool and maintain moisture levels.

This beautiful, antique looking clematis (hybridised in the 1870's by George Jackman & Son) has layers of pointy, silvery-mauve petals which lend it an aura of faded elegance; I was entranced yesterday to pass by and spot a spider's web across one of its flowers. It made me wonder: who was 'Belle of Woking'? A Victorian dowager and patron of horticulture perhaps? Or were George and his son so blown away by its beauty that 'Belle' simply seemed the most fitting name?

I will give the last word to Christopher Lloyd, who wrote that he thought the name would be appropriate to a "gallant old steam locomotive".

Penstemon 'Dark Towers'

beard-tongue 'Dark Towers'

There is a faint lull in our garden in the middle of June; many summer-flowering plants are poised for the next act. However, right now *Penstemon* 'Dark Towers' is the show-stopper. It has been flowering for several weeks already and will continue to do so for many more to come and it is truly eye-catching.

Three or four years ago I decided to test out a few different penstemons, so I bought plug-plants, probably twenty or so different ones. Already, by the second season, 'Dark Towers' had filled the top slot, no question. It is similar to *P.* 'Husker Red' — from the same breeder but definitely superior.

One of the first to flower, it is tall for a penstemon, stately even, and hardy. The rich, deep wine-red foliage is semi-evergreen and perfectly sets off the soft pink tubular flowers which rise to a metre or so and are loved by bees.

I could reel off any number of suitable companion plants, but the soft blue-green foliage of *Thalictrum flavum* with its pale-yellow flowers makes the perfect backdrop and the glaucous purple-blue foliage of *Sedum* 'Red Cauli' also springs to mind, as does *Kniphofia* 'Sunningdale Yellow' with its clear-yellow pokers.

Take cuttings in mid-summer as your friends are bound to want one!

Hemerocallis citrina x ochroleuca

daylily citrina x ochroleuca

What plant shall I choose this week? In the last twenty-four hours I have changed my mind at least three or four times, such is the amazing wealth of flowers in the garden in late June.

Amidst the tumbling profusion of roses, clematis, philadelphus, geraniums and all the rest, the cool poise of *Hemerocallis citrina x ochroleuca* won the day — not least because it stands straight and tall at over 1 metre and does not need staking.

It bears fragrant, pale lemon-yellow flowers and these are held well above the foliage. Unlike many in the genus, the balance between flowers and foliage is good and the leaves are narrow and not overwhelming.

It's hard to go wrong with this daylily; I grow mine alongside rosa mundi, with *Nepeta* 'Walker's Low' at its feet and a vivid pink geranium wandering through the stems.

On Sunday, one of the hottest days of the year, we went to Mottisfont in Hampshire and there another yellow star stood out for me. *Rosa* 'Golden Wings' is a well-known, modern shrub rose, very free-flowering, single, fragrant and clear-yellow; it looked stunning. At 5 foot high and the same across, it's perhaps not so suitable for smaller gardens. Nonetheless, it's a winner.

Aeonium arboreum

houseleek tree

With no hint of even a scattered shower on the horizon and increasingly frenetic morning and evening activity with the watering can, as I rush past my *Aeonium arboreum* I throw it grateful and admiring glances in equal measure and make a mental note to water it in a few days time. With their bold, architectural structure, aeoniums not only make a big aesthetic contribution to the group of plants in pots outside our front door, they also demand very little in return, are drought tolerant, and I can't imagine being without them.

There are many different forms of *Aeonium arboreum*, one of the most striking being 'Zwartkop' which has purple-black leaves. After a few years it becomes almost tree-like but if you run out of space, you can easily chop it back and use these to take cuttings: just break off a few rosettes and pot them up in some gritty compost. As its name suggests, the leaves of *A.* 'Blushing Beauty' are flushed with pink and earlier this year I bought 'Voodoo' which has large purple red rosettes.

Aeoniums love to spend summer outside but must have protection from frost during their dormant months, when they especially dislike overwatering. However, even if you don't have a greenhouse, they are reasonably tolerant of lower light levels and can easily be overwintered in a porch or on a windowsill.

Geranium pratense 'Southease Celestial'

cranesbill 'Southease Celestial'

After I bought this geranium (from the marvellous Marchants Hardy Plants) and watched it transform into a celestial cloud of powder-blue the following year, I felt the need to visit its place of origin. This took me to the tiny village of Southease lying due south of Lewes in East Sussex, tucked away in a beautiful corner of the South Downs National Park.

Southease holds an annual plant fair on the green and also hosts an 'open gardens' day. So, despite its size (population approx. 50) it has many attractions, not least a beautiful 12th century church with a round tower, and it has lent its name to my subject this week.

I can't do better than steal this description from Marchants' catalogue:

"wonderful huge cupped salvers of luminescent lavender-blue". Mine has been in flower since the end of May and, as always, benefits hugely from deadheading. It is not planted under a rose but it would be the perfect companion, as would many geraniums — there's one more item to add to my 'to do' list!

Sadly, not many nurseries supply 'Southease Celestial', so that gives me an excuse to mention another favourite from the family which is *Geranium sanguineum* 'Khan'. Its large dark pink flowers are sumptuous and it has that easy habit of wandering and clambering amongst its neighbours. I wouldn't be without this one either.

Rosa Bonica

modern shrub rose

I've known Bonica for a long time as I first took notice of it in my mother's garden many years ago. She had masses of roses and therefore had that understanding of their ways that can only come from growing them. I remember wondering, when she and my father downsized, how on earth she would choose which roses to grow in their new and much smaller garden. It turned out to be easier than I thought and Bonica was on that list. I not only took note, I took cuttings, one of which is the very plant we grow today — 25 years on!

It is one of the last roses to come into flower but is well worth the wait. It is generous and uncomplicated and always gives of its best. Its dainty sprays of clear pink, lightly scented blooms will continue on and off all summer until the first frosts.

There is very little not to like about Bonica: it's robust, it has good foliage, it's almost disease-free, has good hips in the autumn (just remember to stop deadheading towards the end of summer if you want these), and it is certainly tolerant of some shade. What more could you ask for?

Digitalis ferruginea

rusty foxglove

This foxglove is a jewel. I know I'm on to a winner when each time I pass a plant I find myself stopping and staring at it in wonder and my selection this week is no exception. It is also an absolute magnet for every passing bee which just adds to the interest.

The rusty foxglove is more likely to be a short-lived perennial than a biennial and can be encouraged to behave as one by cutting back the spent stem right down to the basal rosette. However, do leave at least one seedhead and you may be lucky enough to get seedlings.

It is always interesting to see where it has chosen to grow in our garden, as I have read variously that this foxglove likes sun, shade, partial shade, damp, dry, acid, alkaline or neutral. My photograph shows a happy self-seeded specimen, and for us it chose the edge of a gravel path as its home. I couldn't have placed it better myself: nature knows best.

The tiny seedlings are quite distinctive so you will easily spot them. The dark green, long, pointy leaves that make up the rosette are beautifully set out and half the pleasure is in the anticipation of what's to come: tall stately spires (1 to 1.2m) bearing closely packed tubular buds which open to reveal a very unusual golden yellow interior with coppery brown veins. Gorgeous!

Itea ilicifolia

holly-leaved sweet spire

There's no doubt that many herbaceous perennials are suffering in this hot dry spell and although I try to keep watering anything that I have planted this year, those more established plants just have to survive on their own reserves in a larger garden, or simply in the busyness of life.

However, in the shrub category, there are one or two which seem positively to thrive, to glow even: the most obvious in our garden being the not-so-often-encountered *Itea ilicifolia.* This hardy evergreen shrub has fresh, mid-green, holly-shaped leaves and right now it is covered in cool lime-green icicles: exceptionally long and graceful summer catkins which will flower right through to the autumn.

Ours is growing against a west-facing wall because that was the recommendation when we bought it, but it can do well as a stand-alone shrub and will also tolerate a certain amount of shade. It is easy to grow and eventually tall (3m plus). Happy to be pruned in the spring if it outgrows its allotted space, it is one of those shrubs that adapts and intermingles without too much intervention and will soon reward you with a cool summer waterfall — which is something we could all do with right now!

AUGUST

Veronicastrum virginicum 'Erica'

Culver's root 'Erica'

One of the great pleasures towards the end of a holiday is to anticipate my first stroll around the garden upon our return. A week's absence allows us to look at it all with fresh eyes, to enjoy the subtle changes, to notice the first flowers on an old favourite reappearing.

This week *Veronicastrum virginicum* 'Erica' stands out for me, partly because much of the rest of the garden is now in 'green' mode, waiting for the late summer flowers to start in earnest, while 'Erica' is in full-flower. But it is more than just colour: it adds elegance and structure to the whole border and not only are the flowers long-lasting, they age in a most graceful manner.

In early spring the emerging new shoots are red but the stems and foliage only retain a tinge of colour as the season progresses. The upright, slender spires of soft-pink flowers belie the robust nature of the plant. Being compact and not in the least invasive, 'Erica' is very suitable for a small garden, but it is also well able to hold its own in a larger border. It does best in full sun and reaches about 120cm. All veronicastrum associate especially well with grasses and they are a magnet for bees.

Carex testacea

New Zealand hair sedge

Like a constant friend who goes way back, so does my plant this week. I've had it for as long as I can remember, always there in a pot outside the front door giving me pleasure each time I pass by. It's also a terrific foil to other plants.

Evergreen and seemingly never having an off-day, it is the warm and coppery orange leaves that make this grass so compelling, and whose subtle colour changes through each season prevent it from becoming boring. At this time of the year, when the sun's evening rays come slanting through the arching leaves, the entire plant glows as if on fire.

This sedge from New Zealand is the ultimate low-maintenance plant.

Occasionally it needs a tidy-up — a comb through to remove the oldest leaves — and if you aren't lucky enough to find seedlings, you can always lift and divide it (April is best) and get your extra plants that way.

Like many grasses, *C. testacea* needs an open sunny position in well-drained soil and it looks superb in a pot. The rather insignificant flowers arrive in midsummer and this year, for the first time ever, I have found two seedlings in the gravel drive. I shall leave them: invariably self-sown plants position themselves in the perfect spot and repetition in any planting scheme is always good.

Koelreuteria paniculata

pride of India, golden rain tree

That I love propagating all plants goes without saying, but above all I have a particular fondness for trees that I have raised from seed. So much is invested: the collection, the sowing, the waiting, the watching, the watering. Then by magic, or so it seems, a tiny green shoot appears and others soon follow.

A few years ago I was walking through the Cambridgeshire village of Hemingford Grey with my sister, when we stopped in our tracks to admire a beautiful 'golden rain tree' in the churchyard. Instantly I made a mental note to ask Fran to return in a few weeks time to collect some seed.

The showy panicles of flowers (loved by bees) produce an airy haze of clear-yellow in midsummer, followed by interesting seed pods. In the autumn, the ferny foliage turns a wonderful butter-yellow.

Sun is a must and it likes good drainage. I know that to my cost and I wish I had not made a bet with Fran that mine would grow taller and stronger, for I forgot the grit at planting time!

Hylotelephium 'Red Cauli'

previously Sedum 'Red Cauli'
stonecrop 'Red Cauli'

Just to confuse us further, not *all* sedums are re-named *Hylotelephium*, only some of them, but I'm not getting into that discussion here…

Seen here with *Diascia personata* in the background, my star plant this week is the amazing stonecrop 'Red Cauli': it is one of those plants that just sings at this time of the year. Coincidentally, unlike 99% of most plants neither of these two thrives in a pot: the sedum seems to want to grow sideways out of it and the *Diascia* is so brittle that if you pick up the pot you invariably snap off a lovely long flowering stem — they don't make life easy for nursery owners. But once planted, I can hardly think of two plants that better earn their keep in the border.

Introduced by Graham Gough of Marchants Hardy Plants, it was given the 'Award of Garden Merit' by the RHS in 2006. 'Red Cauli' has all the usual characteristics of the genus, but the intense red colouring of its flowerheads in combination with the glaucous green foliage is unbeatable.

This year I decided against the Chelsea chop for my sedums and luckily they are standing up well thanks to a dry summer (height approx. 45cm).

Either way, 'Red Cauli' wins hands down!

Gomphostigma virgatum

otter bush, river star, besembossie

At first glance, this elegant, upright and small shrub looks as if it would revel in a dry, sunny spot — much where you would expect to grow lavender and rosemary. Indeed, you would imagine that its silver-grey leaves and tiny white flowers would sit happily in a typical Mediterranean habitat. Well, it didn't take long to discover that this plant originates in southern Africa and guess what? It mostly grows along riverbanks and watercourses.

I raised my plants from seed and planted them out the following spring. I am ashamed to admit that at the time, I didn't check out their preferred environment and assumed they'd like it sunny and well drained. As it turns out,

they seem to like that too. Having said that, mine have barely reached 1 metre after three years, whereas in their natural habitat they attain 2.6 metres, as quoted on the PlantZAfrica website.

This is a very easy and accommodating shrub and is fast becoming more widely available. It has an open habit and rubs shoulders very happily with many late summer flowering perennials and especially with grasses. It can be pruned back quite hard in early spring, much as you would a buddleia.

It is said that "*Gomphostigma virgatum* is traditionally used to restore strength to a very tired person". Well, that's most of us after a day's gardening!

~

Sanguisorba 'Pink Brushes'

burnet 'Pink Brushes'

Like an eccentric but glamorous great-aunt, my plant this week is a wonderful example of how to age gracefully. Going grey — yes. Losing other attributes — no!

A bit like going to a big family party, I walk into the garden and there she is, you can't miss her — tall, willowy and colourful. I am thrilled with this new addition to my autumn border.

When I first started gardening, I distinctly remember growing salad burnet (*Sanguisorba minor*) in my herb garden. Little did I realise then, what a large, varied and interesting genus it was, but in those days, unlike today, they were seldom used in the border.

Sanguisorba come in many different heights and colours — from white to all hues of pink to deepest burgundy — and the shapes of their flowers, usually held on wiry stems well above the handsome foliage, are variously described as catkins, tassels, bobbles and burrs. 'Pink Brushes' has large fluffy flowers that look a little like huge pink caterpillars.

Just writing about them makes me realise how many I don't yet grow. An interesting way to see them in action would be to go to the RHS Sanguisorba trials* at Wisley. If you don't live in the south, then try visiting Avondale Nursery near Coventry where they hold a national collection.

*Written in September 2018; the Sanguisorba trials at Wisley ended in 2020.

Althaea cannabina

palm-leaf marsh mallow

I'm all for transparency and not just in the late summer or early autumn border! Over the last few weeks I have been looking long and hard at such plantings and have come to the conclusion that relentless clumps of rudbeckia, helenium, eupatorium, persicaria, etc., do not always fit with the average garden plot: appropriate in a prairie planting maybe, or setting off a public building, but many of these plants are simply too dense and hoggish and before you know it there's no room for anything else. The trick is to choose your subjects very carefully indeed; grasses are indispensable at this time of the year, as are certain asters. But again, be selective.

My chosen plant this week is *Althaea cannabina*, a member of the same family as the well loved hollyhock and it illustrates my point perfectly. It flowers from summer through to October with delicate pale-pink flowers with a darker centre and is tall and willowy, though even at 6 or 7 foot it should not need staking. Don't forget to prune it to the ground in late autumn.

It is a real see-through plant and grows happily with late sanguisorba, verbena, veronicastrum, *Molinia caerulea* 'Transparent', *Succisa pratensis, Diascia personata* and countless others. I hate to mention the 'C' word in September, but top of your reading wish list should be Marina Christopher's 'Late Summer Flowers'. She also sells at many plant fairs under the name Phoenix Perennial Plants.

Vitex agnus-castus f. latifolia

broad-leaved chaste tree

I must start by mentioning the garden where I first saw this week's plant. A few years ago, I took my mother on a little garden-visiting jaunt to South Wales and we came across this gem of a place (The Nurtons Garden & Nursery) nestled into a beautiful and secluded valley with breathtaking views. Tucked into the hillside, it was filled with treasures including many salvias and other Mediterranean plants. I saw their *Vitex* in full flower and fell for it.

This unusual shrub is a magnet for bees, butterflies and other insects and bears upright sprays of fragrant, lavender-blue flowers from July, August or September depending upon its location. Buddleias are in flower at the same time, but for me the grey-green foliage of *Vitex* is more attractive and its flowers die more gracefully too. It is hardy to -10°C as long as it has shelter (a south-facing wall or fence is ideal) and good drainage.

A note on pruning: *Vitex* can be left untouched and in which case will attain 4 metres plus. However, a hard prune in early spring will keep it to a size more appropriate for the average garden.

Plectranthus argentatus

silver spur flower

Plectranthus are members of the *Lamiaceae*, or mint, family and they're my latest craze. All species are tender and are valuable subjects for those keen on container growing, not only for the highly ornamental value of their foliage but also because many are happiest grown in part shade and some in almost full shade. Even *P. argentatus*, with its silver-grey leaves (which usually indicates a love of undiluted sunshine), does best for me with a little shade especially at the hottest time of the day.

The soft velvety leaves alone are reason enough to give it pride of place in any scheme, but nonetheless I always look forward to the quiet spikes of palest purple flowers at the end of the summer and so do the bees.

The silver spur flower, as it's commonly known, is at its peak right now and with a bit of luck will continue to look good for at least another four or five weeks. This goes for almost all tender plants in containers: they have been building up to this fabulous autumn crescendo and it rarely disappoints.

Last year there was a widespread frost at the end of October and *P. argentatus* was the first to succumb. However, the good news is that it is one of the very easiest to propagate and this year I am going to try cuttings in a glass of water: a method which is not only fun but also works well for so many plants.

We have just had our first very early, light frost in the garden this week — -0.5°C!

OCTOBER

Diascia personata

masked twinspur

For me this is the ultimate cottage garden plant. It can get overlooked in the summer as there is so much competition, but in actual fact I could have chosen the lovely *Diascia personata* for this slot at any time from late spring until the end of October. This week it looks simply stunning surrounded by grasses, asters, a blue salvia, and the fading, autumnal flowerheads of almost everything else.

D. personata is a short-lived, semi-evergreen, hardy perennial (H4 but must have sun and good drainage) and it grows happily alongside almost any border companion. The dusky-pink flowers have a dark centre and are borne on tall, upright stems that need no staking. It is the very unusual hue of this *Diascia* that makes it so attractive to me, especially in the autumn; the pink is not in the least strident and never seems to clash with anything. The other great bonus is that it absolutely does not need deadheading.

I cannot close without a mention of cuttings because you never know what the winter is going to throw at you. So long as there is green on the plant, you can take them and at almost any time of the year, you will be successful using the water method.

Once you have *Diascia personata*, you will never want to be without it.

Symphyotrichum ericoides 'Deep Danziger'

...and other asters

There are certain genera that simply must be seen in flower before you buy them and *Symphyotrichum* is firmly on that list. It is oh-so-easy to be swayed by glowing descriptions on labels or in catalogues, only to find that the colour or height, or both, weren't quite what you were expecting, or that the habit is disappointing. There is no substitute for seeing the actual plant, talking to the person who has grown it and there is no better place to do that than at a good plant fair. One of the best, certainly in the south of England, is held at Great Dixter garden biannually and the autumn event has just taken place.

I'm going to mention a few other asters here because despite ticking all the boxes, sadly 'Deep Danziger' is not widely available. I bought it from Marina Christopher of Phoenix Perennial Plants, who in turn, found it in a French nursery called Le Domaine de la Source (they sometimes also exhibit at Great Dixter alongside Marina).

A stunning white aster that I also bought from Phoenix Perennial Plants is 'Monte Cassino'. Loved by flower arrangers, it has strong upright stems bedecked with clouds of tiny white flowers. Another favourite is 'Alma Potschke', which has vivid cerise-pink flower heads and everyone will vouch for 'Little Carlow', including the RHS ('Award of Garden Merit') — it isn't exactly small (90cm) but forms a mound of almost luminous lavender-blue flowers. Last but by no means least is *A. peduncularis which is* not so easily sourced because it is tricky to propagate — or so I've heard. However, it is well worth seeking out because the colour of the mauve-blue flower is exceptional and the plant itself is robust and adaptable.

As is the magic of this season, somehow *all* of these colours get along together in the autumn border.

Serratula tinctoria var. seoanei

It is often said of plants that they 'should be more widely used' or that they are 'not often seen in gardens'. It could be tempting to say the same of my choice this week, but I am pretty sure I know the reason behind its elusiveness: it is at its peak in October, and often into November, and so it's not going to make many sales in nurseries and even less in garden centres at this time of year. Rather, the plant buying public are turning their thoughts to spring bulbs or — dare I mention — the forthcoming festive season!

This late-flowering, hardy member of the aster family is well worth seeking out. It is often described as thistle-like or a knapweed, but please don't let this put you off because it is a trusty and robust little plant that has a season way beyond its flowers. The RHS describes it as 'compact and poised' and this is spot on!

Excellent towards the front of the border, in a naturalistic or gravel garden, and very good in combination with grasses. The foliage is neat, dark green, and very dissected, almost like a fern, while the upright, wiry stems hold masses of pinky-mauve flowers which bear little 'antennae' among the petals. Then come the delightful seedheads and on no account cut these down because throughout the winter from December right up until March, and especially under frost, the old skeleton will give you almost as much pleasure as when the plant is in full flower. If you don't go round your garden much in the winter, then plant it not too far from the front door, or where you can see it from a window.

Ageratina ligustrina

privet-leaved ageratina

This unusual, autumn–flowering shrub used to be known as *Eupatorium ligustrinum* and for once I am happy to see a plant renamed. *Eupatorium* are known to be a faintly thuggish lot and the idea of one with privet type leaves was not appealing. However, *Ageratina ligustrina* is neither thuggish, nor does it bear anything but a passing resemblance to a privet.

Above shiny, neat, slightly pointy leaves, the flat heads of tiny, white flowers cover this dainty evergreen shrub from September through to October and on sunny days butterflies and bees will descend en masse to enjoy one of their last late season feasts.

A. ligustrina originates from Mexico and parts of Central America and will need a sheltered position to give of its best: south– or west–facing and preferably against a wall. In a really severe winter it could succumb, especially if the soil is anything less than well drained. However, cuttings really are easy so this is always a good insurance policy. A hard prune in the spring, as for a buddleja, is almost all it will ask of you.

Chrysanthemum 'Innocence'

For years I fought against growing chrysanthemums, probably influenced by their association with funerals and by those garish bunches wrapped in coloured cellophane on garage forecourts. However, recently and particularly after growing 'Innocence', I have come to appreciate their contribution to our garden at what can be rather a sombre time of year; who would not enjoy the soft, pink-tinged white flowers that welcome me each time I step out of the back door? Flowers that have, last week, weathered and come sailing through −2.8°C.

'Innocence' is one of the single Korean chrysanthemums, which have been bred over many years to more than earn their place in our gardens today. They are not to be confused with florists' varieties nor with those that adorn the benches at competitions. These hardy types bring unstinting colour to the seriously late autumnal border, long after most other flowers have faded away. They also associate well with grasses, whose foliage and seedheads are by now turning all shades of yellow, orange and rust.

'Innocence' has a wonderful upright habit (70-90cm), its stems are well branched, and it doesn't flop. This year I have grown it in a pot, which means that I have been able to place it exactly where we will get maximum enjoyment.

Darmera peltata

umbrella plant

Now, I realise that the photograph of my chosen plant this week may not be everyone's idea of a horticultural beauty, but with each year that passes I become more fascinated with the seasonal change that is autumn. There is an allure beyond the beauty of vivid colour; gentle decay can also be a fascinating, eye-catching process and the umbrella plant illustrates this perfectly.

Darmera peltata has a long season of interest. It is a vigorous, hardy, herbaceous perennial (growing to about 1m) which is happiest in damp or boggy soil, preferably on the edge of a pond. It is in this position that it is most striking and not just in the autumn; in April and May, domed heads of bright mid-pink flowers

are borne on tall, naked stems well before the foliage appears and their reflections in the water below serve to accentuate their architectural splendour.

Then come the leaves: huge, shaped like parasols with scalloped edges, and shiny green until they start to turn all shades of yellow, orange, and red in September. *Darmera peltata* is probably the best alternative for those who'd love to grow *Gunnera manicata* but simply don't have the room. Its dense rhizomes spread slowly and surely but you couldn't call it invasive. The ultimate 'no maintenance' plant, I don't even tidy it up in the winter; it self-mulches and will be ready to go next spring.

Panicum virgatum 'Northwind'

switch grass 'Northwind'

Each autumn brings subtly different colour schemes to the last and it all depends on the sun, wind, rain, and frost, and the order in which they come and go throughout the year. Some plants excel, where before they were more muted.

This week it's the turn of an American switch grass, 'Northwind' — it has been grabbing my attention for the last few weeks until I could no longer ignore it. It is best placed in full sun where the clear autumn sunlight can stream through the hues of golden yellow, orange, and tan. In our garden I grow it alongside *Salvia* 'Phyllis Fancy', *Chrysanthemum* 'Cottage Apricot' and *Verbena bonariensis*.

Panicum virgatum 'Northwind' is the most narrowly upright form of the genus and is therefore perfect for the smaller border where other grasses might elbow out their less pushy neighbours. 'Northwind' is clump-forming and as a single specimen it makes a stunning vertical accent. It grows to about 150cm, doesn't flop, is tolerant of most soils and remains neat throughout the winter. In March, cut down the stems to ground level and chop them up as you go, leaving them behind as a mulch.

In 2014 it won the Perennial Plant Association's 'Perennial Plant of the Year'.

102

Malus hupehensis

Hupeh crab

The tree in the photo is not actually in our garden. About twenty-five years ago, our neighbour, who grew it from seed, planted it on the verge in our lane and I still watch its progress through the seasons from the kitchen window.

Ernest Wilson discovered it in central China where people make tea from its leaves, giving it its other common name, the tea crab apple. Apparently, he considered it to be the finest deciduous tree he introduced into this country and indeed it gives us pleasure on so many fronts.

The show starts in around April or May when the delicate pink buds open to a profusion of white flowers which have a subtle musky scent; it makes a simply stunning display and passing walkers often stop by to ask its name.

For me, the best comes in the autumn. The small round fruits start to turn colour and eventually hang red, like cherries, from the branches. Simultaneously the leaves turn to yellow to ochre to rust; the combination is breathtaking. Then come the birds, it is their autumn feast. The tree is besieged by large flocks of fieldfares and redwings — and probably many others — and the accompanying sound is magic.

It would be the perfect choice for a specimen in the middle of a lawn, however, it's not a tree for a small garden as it reaches 6 to 8 metres over time. Failing that, you too could try a bit of guerrilla gardening...

DECEMBER

Euphorbia x pasteurii
'John Phillips'

spurge 'John Phillips'

In the summer months, evergreen shrubs are mostly background, but when winter comes, they are backbone; from now on, they become more and more important as the last remaining leaves of deciduous plants fall to earth.

Coloured stems, bare twigs, and silhouettes of trees, all play their part in the winter garden, as do the many highly scented flowers that come into their own as the new year unfolds; but right now, the evergreen shrubs hold centre stage and none does it better than my special plant this week.

It is a truly garden-worthy plant: architectural, robust, and vigorous. Being part child of *E. mellifera*, it has the bonus, in summer, of delicious honey-scented flowers. It is, however, different from its parent plant in many respects: its foliage is a darker green with a strong, central, pale midrib, and it easily reaches 160cm high and the same or more across. Its second parent is *E. stygiana*, an interesting but less vigorous euphorbia whose lower leaves turn brilliant red in winter; but this one has never really thrived on our cold dank clay and seems to be asking to be returned to the Azores asap!

All we need now is a frost, which turns *E. x pasteurii* 'John Phillips' into a true winter wonder.

Echeveria rosea

Almost all *Echeveria* will succumb to winter wet and cold in the UK, but not this one, not unless we have a particularly extreme season. It is easily the most able to cope with whatever weather is thrown at it.

All succulents look great in containers, whether grown as single specimens or in mixed groups but by the end of the summer difficult choices have to be made. For unless you have a very large greenhouse you will be hard-pressed to find room for all the tender treasures. This is one good reason why *E. rosea* is worth seeking out, it positively needs to be outside in the cold.

I was therefore very excited to come across this stunning succulent (bought from Bob Brown at Cotswold Garden Flowers) which positively gives of its best, the colder it gets. From now until late winter the whole plant will gradually turn an eye-catching red, at which point the flower buds will start to form. The flowers are somewhere between coral-red and yellow.

A final reminder that free-draining soil is essential, which translates as loads of gravel or grit in the potting mix. Mine grows in a pot by the front door which is where I can enjoy its every nuanced change.

Chimonanthus praecox

wintersweet

Wintersweet is without doubt the most striking plant in our garden this month. Striking, not only because it is so heavily laden with flowers this year — I am wondering how this happened after such a mediocre summer — but also because its fragrance is pure heaven.

Planted in 1990, it was one of the best choices we made, even though initially I began to doubt it, as several winters passed before the unusual waxy flowers started to appear, along with their intoxicating scent.

The name translates from Greek as 'precocious' (or 'early') 'winter flower' and, as the name suggests, for the rest of the year you wouldn't give it a second glance, so a little bit of thought is needed to extend its season of interest. We planted a late flowering form of *Clematis cirrhosa* var. *balearica* which has greenish creamy bells and no freckles. It is just starting into bud as I write and will take over from the wintersweet towards the end of the winter, draping itself over the crown like a sort of floral parasol. This is followed, in early summer, by *Clematis* 'Gillian Blades' which has large, single, snowy white flowers and meanders gracefully through the lower twigs of the *Chimonanthus*.

I could get carried away with ideas for underplanting but the thought of snowdrops has reminded me that I need to ice the Christmas cake, so in the meantime — if you are celebrating — have a happy one!

Erysimum 'Parish's'

wallflower 'Parish's'

December can be short on flowers. Early bulbs, sweet scented winter flowering shrubs, and most hellebores come into their own from January onwards; but for this time of the year, my subject this week is in a class of its own. I can honestly say that there is hardly a month throughout the year when it is not in flower. Don't imagine that it is nestled against a south facing sheltered wall, nor is it in a pot tucked well up against the house; our garden is cold and yet this wallflower still flourishes with us in an open bed, admittedly a very well drained one.

Erysimum 'Parish's' is a hardy, low-growing, evergreen wallflower with bright magenta-purple flowers. I was going to use the word 'sprawling' to characterise its habit but remember seeing it once described as 'curtseying' and I can't do better than that.

'Parish's' associates well with smaller grasses and low-growing, grey-leaved sub-shrubs. Next autumn I shall plant some spring bulbs around its base as these would thrive happily amidst its open growth. Being relatively short-lived, it responds well to light pruning when it gets too leggy.

We're not far off the shortest day and for me there is no plant quite so plucky as *Helleborus niger* and there is no better place for it than in a pot beside the front door. You will be enthralled long after the Christmas decorations have come down...

Index of Scientific and common names

113

Notes